BARRON'S Let's Prepare for the
PARCC
GRADE 7 MATH TEST

Kristen Scott, M.S.
Mathematics Teacher and Assistant Principal
Wall Township School District
Wall, New Jersey

About the Author

Kristen Scott, M.S., is the current assistant principal at Wall High School. Prior to that, she was a STEM supervisor, a STEM curriculum assistant for grades K–8, and a high school math teacher. Her area of expertise is in the Common Core, standardized testing, and mathematical instruction. Kristen obtained her master's degree from Scranton University in Educational Administration. She also holds a B.A. in mathematics from Rowan University. She has been training teachers on the Common Core Standards and the PARCC Assessment for the past four years.

Acknowledgments

Many thanks to:

The loves of my life for making me all who I am: ES, GS, ES, BS, IS.

The ones who fill me with knowledge and support: OJ, MW, JJJ.

All the dedicated teachers and administrators of the Wall Township School District.

My nephews for keeping it real!

In memory of Gene Johnson: A beloved math teacher and father.

7/15 changed my life and 5/5 changed it back.

All inquiries should be addressed to:
Barron's Educational Series, Inc.
250 Wireless Boulevard
Hauppauge, NY 11788
www.barronseduc.com

ISBN: 978-1-4380-0820-2

Library of Congress Control Number 2016936362

Date of Manufacture: August 2016
Manufactured by: B11R11

Printed in the United States of America
9 8 7 6 5 4 3 2 1

10%
POST-CONSUMER
WASTE
Paper contains a minimum
of 10% post-consumer
waste (PCW). Paper used
in this book was derived
from certified, sustainable
forestlands.

Contents

Chapter 4
The Number System 41

Chapter 5
Expressions and Equations 73

Chapter 6
Geometry 111

Chapter 7
Statistics and Probability 155

PARCC Reference Sheet

1 inch = 2.54 centimeters
1 meter = 39.37 inches
1 mile = 5,280 feet
1 mile = 1,760 yards
1 mile = 1.609 kilometers

1 kilometer = 0.62 miles
1 pound = 16 ounces
1 pound = 0.454 kilograms
1 kilogram = 2.2 pounds
1 ton = 2,000 pounds

1 cup = 8 fluid ounces
1 pint = 2 cups
1 quart = 2 pints
1 gallon = 4 quarts
1 gallon = 3.785 liters
1 liter = 0.264 gallons
1 liter = 1,000 cubic
    centimeters

Triangle	$A = (\frac{1}{2}) bh$
Parallelogram	$A = bh$
Circle	$A = \pi r^2$
Circle	$C = \pi d$ or $C = 2\pi r$
General prisms	$V = Bh$

PARCC Calculator Policy

The PARCC Mathematics Assessment for Grade 7 will allow for an online four function calculator with square root. The PARCC is divided into calculator and non-calculator sessions, provided that the other sessions of the assessment are locked. The same calculator with maximum functionality is to be used for all items on calculator sessions.

Test-Taking Strategies

The majority of students will take the PARCC as a computer-based assessment. The strategies listed below are for students who will be taking the online version of the assessment. For students with accommodations that allow for a paper-and-pencil version of the PARCC Assessment, make sure you practice the paper-and-pencil version available at *www.parcconline.org* so that you are comfortable with the bubbling answer procedures.

General Strategies

- Pay attention to details.
- When problem solving, ask yourself what are you being asked to find.
- Be confident.
- Always read the whole question carefully.
- Use all the scratch paper you want (this is allowed as an accessibility feature).
- Don't worry if others finish before you; the estimated time per task is less than the time you have to take the assessment.
- Listen attentively to the general instructions.
- Eliminate unlikely answers first (see *Eliminating Answer Choices* on page 10).
- Don't panic (you've got this).
- Don't get stuck on a problem for too long (see *Flagging Questions* on page 11).
- Don't press the Submit button until you have completed all answers.

Major Work of the Grade

The PARCC Assessment defines, for each grade, the major, additional, and supporting Common Core Standards. More than 60% of the questions on the PARCC will focus on the standards for seventh grade that are labeled as the major work for the grade. If students are comfortable with the major work of the seventh-grade Mathematics Common Core Standards, they will be comfortable tackling the majority of problems on the PARCC.

The major work for seventh grade, as defined by the Common Core State Standards Initiative (*www.corestandards.org*), consists of students developing, solving, and drawing inferences:

- "Developing understanding of and applying proportional relationships"
- "Developing understanding of operations with rational numbers and working with expressions and linear equations"
- "Solving problems involving scale drawings and informal geometric constructions, and working with two- and three-dimensional shapes to solve problems involving area, surface area, and volume"
- "Drawing inferences about populations based on samples"

Grading Procedures

- Questions on the seventh-grade PARCC that are worth more than one point will have more of the points assigned to the explanation. The reasoning, modeling, and/or application aspect of the problems will be worth more points, and the correct response will be worth fewer points. Students can come up with the wrong answer and still earn points for their reasoning or modeling.
- Final scores on the PARCC Assessment will reflect each student's performance on all mathematics units taken. Although the units may be taken at separate times in the PARCC testing window, students will not receive a separate score for each individual unit.
- Rubrics aligned to the PARCC Performance Level Descriptors will detail the requirements for a student's response. A question could have multiple rubrics. For example, a question worth 4 points could have a Part A worth 2 points and a Part B worth 2 points or Part A may be only worth 1 point, while Part B is worth 3 points. Most released rubrics for the PARCC have shown that a question worth 3 points will have 3 elements. If a student answers all 3 correctly, he or she will receive the 3 points; if a student's response includes 2 of the 3 elements, he or she will receive 2 points, and so forth.
- Answers can be in any equivalent form of a solution unless specifically stated in the problem or question.
- Partial credit will be given on some PARCC seventh-grade mathematics questions. These questions will be predetermined to receive partial credit. The range of credit will be decided when reviewing sets of real student work after the assessment is complete.

Fluency

The seventh-grade Common Core Standards do have specific fluency standards; however, they will not be tested the way they are in the younger PARCC-tested grade levels. In the earlier grades, fluency is tested for accuracy and speed in the non-calculator section. The seventh-grade fluency standards and the grades above are included on the PARCC Assessment but are not tested as a specific fluency component.

   For example, one of the fluency standards for seventh graders is Common Core Standard EE.B.4, which asks students to solve one-variable equations of the form $px + q = r$ and $p(x + q) = r$ fluently. Even though students won't be tested specifically as to whether they perform this standard quickly and accurately, it will be a key aspect for students to have had sufficient practice with so they can *apply* this skill in various problems.

Question Types

Multiple-Choice vs. Multiple-Select

Knowing whether there is one answer for a question or whether there are multiple answers can be extremely valuable and helpful. The verbiage in the questions on the PARCC will generally state this, but there is also something else you can watch out for. Multiple-choice questions have only one answer, and the answer choices will begin with a circle.

Which equation has a constant of proportionality equal to 4?

○　A. $4y = 4x$

○　B. $4y = 12x$

○　C. $3y = 4x$

○　D. $3y = 12x$

Multiple-select questions can have more than one answer and will have answer choices that begin with a square.

A right triangle has legs measuring 4.5 meters and 1.5 meters.

The lengths of the legs of a second triangle are proportional to the lengths of the legs of the first triangle.

Which could be the lengths of the legs of the second triangle?

Select **each** correct pair of lengths.

☐ A. 6 m and 2 m

☐ B. 8 m and 5 m

☐ C. 7 m and 3.5 m

☐ D. 10 m and 2.5 m

☐ E. 11.25 m and 3.75 m

Drag-and-Drop

Drag-and-drop is another feature that can be practiced with the online assessment tools on *www.parcconline.org*. Click and hold the characters that you are trying to drop. Use caution when placing because, in some problems, the order will matter.

The amount of money Jamie earns is proportional to the number of hours she works. Jamie earns $62.50 working 5 hours.

Create an equation that models the relationship between *m*, the amount of money Jamie earns, in dollars, and *h*, the number of hours she works.

Drag and drop the appropriate number and variables into each box.

| 12.05 | 12.50 | 57.50 | 67.50 | *m* | *h* |

[ ] = [ ] · [ ]

Drop-Down

A drop-down question requires students to select the arrow next to each answer option to view the available response choices. Select from the list to provide the best response.

A 4 $\frac{1}{2}$ -ounce hamburger patty has 25 $\frac{1}{2}$ grams of protein, and 6 ounces of fish has 32 grams of protein. Determine the grams of protein per ounce for each type of food.

Select from the drop-down menus to correctly complete each statement.

A hamburger patty has approximately [Choose... ▾] grams of protein per ounce.

The fish has approximately [Choose... ▾] grams of protein per ounce.

Fill-in-the-Blank

There are two types of responses that require an equation editor. The basic equation editor allows for students to type only math responses. The open-ended response equation editor allows for math plus text. Each equation editor offers quick tools and additional tools. Below, you will find a sample of a math-only equation editor where the additional tools are located below the response box.

The numbers of parts produced by three different machines are shown in the table.

Numbers of Machine Parts

Minutes	Machine Q	Machine R	Machine S
1	9	8	6
3	18	24	18
9	72	72	52

Only one of the machines produces parts at a constant rate. Write an equation that can be used to represent y, the number of parts produced in x minutes, for that machine.

Enter your equation in the space provided. Enter **only** your equation.

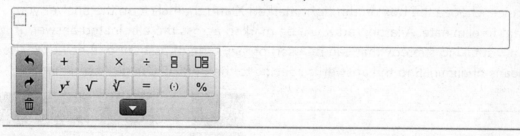

Equation Editor

If you are trying to type in an answer that is a fraction or a decimal and there is just a box there and not the equation editor…guess what? Your answer is not correct. Check your solution by substituting it back into the problem, and you should find you have made a mistake.

The equation editor will be there if the answer requires the equation editor for any reason. If the equation editor is not there, then your answer will fit in the space provided. PARCC offers a free tutorial on using the equation editor at

parcc.pearson.com/tutorial

There are two different equation editors that will be displayed on the seventh-grade PARCC Mathematics Assessment. One of the boxes will be there if the answer only involves an algebraic or numeric expression or equation. Another box will be there if the answer also involves an explanation or words.

Be sure to practice the equation editor that is specifically for sixth through eighth graders, since the equation editor is different for students younger than sixth grade and older than eighth grade. Using this practice run will teach you many important features including how to delete your whole answer, undo the delete, type in absolute value signs and radicals, and practice typing from the keyboard versus the equation editor.

Eliminating Answer Choices

Usually while taking the PARCC Mathematics Assessment, your cursor will be on the arrow below (labeled "Pointer"). However, if you want to eliminate an answer choice, choose the box on the right marked X and then click on the answer you want to eliminate. A large, red X will be marked across the eliminated answer. This is a test-taking strategy that can be used on any type of assessment; however, the means of eliminating the answer is specific to the PARCC Online Assessment.

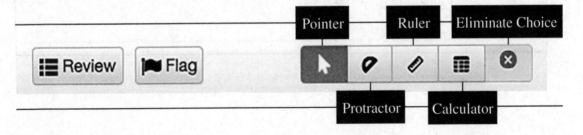